Love you forever

There is someone special in my soulful life
who provides me with such wondrous support
For you are my guiding, glowing, golden angel
who effectively makes my life so easy to sort

In all the lives and years we've known each other
we have never been at each others throats
For the love that glows from your sparkling eyes
stimulates my every trek across relentless moats

For you are the source of my dreams and aspirations
and your love steers me through all my catastrophes
and fills me with such sheer hope and pure vision
that I am totally contented on my eternal journeys

Sometimes when I hold you so very, very close
the world disappears into the shimmering twilight
As our excited souls merge into one loving fusion
the feeling of together forever is remarkably right.

Story Index

Picture Index

Introduction

This is an abundance of intrigue that can infiltrate your very soul. For the reading of many tales, leaves you in no doubt, that love is in the heart of most stories.

Love is unique. It can alter the conception and direction of your life, for there are so many strains of love. It can be for living in Cornwall, visiting special places, music, being with friends, involvement in your favourite pastimes, but then love can grow deeper with feelings for your parents, your children and the one of your dreams. For love can overcome all the problems of life, it can give your body strength and your mind contentment. It can also give your life such depth, but because of its power, it can also destroy you.

So let us now explore the effect of love in Sacred Cornwall.

Thomas Hardy

This exciting, inventive author and poet, born in Dorset, was greatly influenced by Cornwall, exploring the county, its legends and the meeting of a charming and interesting lady, who lived in a rectory, near Tintagel, and who he eventually married.

The writer was born in 1840, at Bockhampton, near Dorchester, Dorset, and after performing very well at school, started to work with his father, but his promising potential was soon detected by a local architect, who offered him an apprenticeship. Based in an office in Dorchester, he was now able to meet people, who would eventually influence his writing. As for romance, there were plenty he met, but he kept everyone at a distance, although he had more than just total admiration for many.

In his early twenties, he finished his apprenticeship, and committed himself to the occupation of assistant architect in London. In this city he had to overcome the different environment, the absent of friends and the many tempting inducements. He explored the many theatres, galleries and dance halls, before progressing with his writing, and sent to the newspapers many poems, which were unfortunately declined. By the age of 25, he was feeling rejected and depressed, and wondered if he would ever be involved with a romantically loving seductive lady. Over the next years his health waned, because of the awful living conditions, mainly due to the lack of the city's drainage, which left an evil smelling river. Also he spent a long time, writing and reading, while his architect work was in danger of becoming depressive, because it included preparation for the expansion of the railway, which went through churchyards and led to the moving of decomposed coffins.

From a young age, he was always involved with the church, and in fact at one time, he wanted to explore the road to ministry. On returning to Dorchester, for a holiday break, his old employer was looking for an employee to plan successful church restorations. The author applied for this immediately, and was accepted. Consequently, he was soon back into his old routine, using his London experience to improve his ability. His health improved quickly.

His book writing was still in the early stages, and he was trying to establish his name and gain the interest of publishers. However his career as an architect gained him a good income. Unfortunately, his employer sadly died, but the new owner gave him a secured employment, which softened the blow, as the next church restoration was in Cornwall, and this visit changed his life.

The church was near Tintagel, and the train journey ended in Launceston, before hir-

ing a horse and cart for the last 16 miles. He arrived in the Rectory after the sun had disappeared for the night. With the vicar ill in bed and his wife comforting him, the visitor was greeted at the door by the vicar's sister-in-law, Emma, an inspiring, attractive lady, who over the next months gradually drew him into her love web, and he unashamedly fell for her. Tintagel is a very romantic location, which allows your love to flourish in gorgeous surroundings, roaming ravishing coast paths of exquisite beauty, hand in hand, encountering secluded areas, which grants you time to explore each others love.

"Far from the Madding Crowd" was the book, that brought his initial success and fame. It was conceived and fashioned during his courting of Emma, and published just after their marriage. So her influence had been major in his success.

However as their marriage continued, so the love floated away, due to the author being so absorbed in his writing, which often left his wife outside his world. Despite this remoteness, that existed between the two, their marriage continued for a period longer than most, until one day Emma decided to play all her favourite tunes on her piano, and when finished, went to bed and gradually faded away from this life.

This just devastated Thomas, for it soon became apparent to him, how much he missed her, and he was angry with himself for not bridging the gap between them. In the past, when alive, Emma had been a major inspiration in his life, now due to her death, he found the grief difficult to control. Wandering around cliff places in Cornwall, where they had rambled together, he heard her voice in the windy background, and then wrote the most incredible love poems possible. For even withdrawn from his life, Emma could motivate the author to a very high level of composing.

He lived for another 16 years, to the age of 87, and married a much younger lady than himself. Her name was Florence, who had helped him with his manuscripts and was a friend of Emma. Thomas had accepted awards for his work, and contributed articles to assist the soldiers during the First World War, but he was still downhearted by the loss of his first wife, and spent time in Cornwall, visiting places where he and Emma had been inseparable, lost in love, their spirits flying high above the clouds.

But at the end of the day, he regretted there was only a short happy period in their marriage, and wished she was back in his arms. However he was able to spend the end of his life still alert, given good support by Florence, and as he left us, he still was unable to decide whether his life had been worthwhile, but his readers certainly found his work exciting and inventive.

A Cornish Parents' Love Story

Saint Barnabas Hospital in Saltash, will always linger in my heart, not because I was born there, but this is the place where my parents' love started. Just after the second World War, when Saltash main street was devastated by the German bombing, there was a feeling of bubbling excitement in the nation, with the resounding victory, having overcome the severe stress of the war, which could have destroyed the way of the world.

The future was engrossed in a substantial level of hope and contentment. Buying food was restricted with coupons, and the reconstruction of buildings was immense. Many families had lost loved ones, and life had changed dramatically, but now the air was clear, and the sun warmed the world, cleansing the atmosphere of terror and imminent fear of loss of life that existed for many years. It enforced the view, that good will always overcome evil, but the effort needed can be very extreme.

The year had advanced to when the spring period was eroding the bleak winter, days of glorious sunshine, the emerging of the glowing daffodils, and the awakening of hibernating animals. At the hospital, a very attractive lady had joined the staff, after attending school at Callington and Saltash, and then, working for a period at Ince Castle, where her father was head gardener until the 1970s.

The gardener at the hospital was previously a sergeant major in the Army, and had served several years in India. His son had overcome the effect of no education, until the family had arrived back in Cornwall when he was nine, and rose rapidly to the top class at school. When he left school he became an apprentice woodworker, and joined the Navy just prior to the Second World War.

During the war, he had been part of the Navy protecting the Merchant Navy on the way to Malta, where the ships were under constant bombardment for several days. He had witnessed the ship next to his, being totally destroyed as a bomb hit their ammunition store, and only 3 sailors survived. Another route saw the ship patrol an area of one million square miles, one thousand miles along the equator, down to the Antarctic, endure a thousand miles in the freezing cold before going back to the searing heat of the equator. During the war, he gained many medals and became a local Cornish hero.

His father told him of the good-looking lady, he had seen at the hospital, and their fortunate meeting in the beautiful scenic hospital garden was the start of a lovely romantic marriage of almost fifty years. They married in Saltash, and honeymooned in

Penzance, and danced to the top song of the time, "The Woody Woodpecker" , but loved "When smoke gets in your eyes".

Their woodwork business thrived successfully for 35 years, and the perfectly built furniture will last a long time, for his skill was difficult to master. But now they have left us. The lady suffered for 5 years after losing her love. Together they had walked in Victoria Gardens, Saltash in the late spring sunshine, and his last words were to suggest they sat on a bench in the sun. However a sudden heart attack brutally stopped that proposal.

Now their souls are harmoniously together, which from my grieving point of view is more important and helps me overcome the problem of never seeing them again in this life. I have gained strength with the memory of their story of love etched forever in my heart.

Love can overcome all the problems in the world. It makes the need for money and power pale into insignificance. Love is forever and ever.

King Arthur

When the name King Arthur comes to mind, there is a struggle from within, as though the soul has the answer to the mystery, but the mind is unable to comprehend the meaning. The story of the legend is indelible in the memory, a romantic age of chivalry, of knights in shining armour, performing heroic deeds, remaining in respect and displaying supreme courtesy for the favour of beautiful, graceful ladies dressed in long flowing exquisite gowns. Modern day values seem insufficient and pale before their quests of honour.

The area around Tintagel is the fabled home of King Arthur and his Knights of the Round Table, and on escaping to the island of the legend, there exists a quality that is difficult to define. Breathtaking views, of mighty waves crashing repeatedly, on rugged rocks. The smell of salt water carried by the prevailing wind, intermingled with the sounds of calls from a time gone by. The imagination starts to take over, as inspired by these rare feelings, the visitor glimpses what might have been.

The legend is the basis for many fictional love stories, and the uncontrollable love feelings between Guinevere and Launcelot grew more and more intense, until it demolished King Arthur and Guinevere's marriage. Eventually, leading to the King's death and his sword's return to the Lady of the Lake.

But no matter how many theories are put forward by eminent scholars, who delve deep, there seems no way that the mystery of King Arthur will be revealed. Fact or fiction, the truth is lost behind the mists of time, again and again eluding our grasp. Yet if the mystery was solved, would we really want that, for surely then, the greatest legend ever told would be no more.

Kitty

A shimmering breeze of encroaching warmth, with blue glittering skies and golden captivating sunshine, made Bodmin Moor seem like paradise. For across this adventurous haven rode a very attractive lady with long locks of golden hair that cascaded down to her slim and elegant waist. Her characteristic hunting horse galloped mile after mile, the lady enjoyed the journeys and felt totally protected by this strong panting beast.

This was a time of almost a century ago, when this divine lady, was deeply in love with a Captain, who ran a successful mining business on the moors. They met in Bristol, Kitty, was unaware that her lover was married. His wife, after falling ill was ordered by the doctor to go abroad to recover. After their meeting, Kitty was transported to Sacred Cornwall, a place firmly in her romantic dreams, to live with the Captain and soon became a special friend to all of the local people.

However the secret of the Captain's wife was kept in the misty background, until he was told she was returning. He had no courage to tell Kitty, so a neighbouring lady was left with the heartbreaking disclosure. Kitty was devastated. She collapsed and burst into an overwhelming wail of tears. She ran into the garden, wondering how to escape. The thought of losing the Captain had never entered her mind, as she knew her parents would be unable to accept her relationship. She collapsed. Kitty said her only evasion was suicide, but was whisked away by the neighbour, and quickly she was found somewhere to work and live.

The day before the departure, Kitty decided to say goodbye to the Captain, which left the neighbour very concerned and she advised against it. But Kitty was determined to visit her love, and so her friend gave in, and sent her son with her. The lady was dressed in black and looked very focused. Venturing near the house, she asked the son if she could journey the final distance alone, to see the Captain. The mist descended, engulfing the area into total darkness. The son waited for many hours, but

after thinking Kitty was spending the night with the Captain, decided to return home due to suffering from the cold damp which surrounded him.

Alarmed by her son's return alone, the neighbouring lady travelled quickly to the Captain's house, and found Kitty was nowhere to be seen. The Captain had been unable to believe her when she told him that Kitty was considering suicide, but now it was beginning to become a reality. The distressed neighbour went home, unable to search the pits because of the dark, but after several sleepless pessimistic hours, the inevitable happened, and Kitty's body was discovered in the obvious place.

Kitty had stood on the edge of a seemingly bottomless pit, for her suffering mind was in a grievous state, and having lost her love and accepted there was nowhere to go, the meaning for living had disappeared, and she just leapt to erase her presence in this world.

The Captain on discovering the inevitable, lost his purpose for life, and soon moved from the moors. Kitty was buried at Bolventor Church, near Jamaica Inn, on a very sad day, which left the many mourners encased in grief. So the love story ended in total heartbreak, and left many people in a very morbid mood, but it showed how the loss of love can end in death.

The Last Day in Cornwall

Having lived in Cornwall for so long, I knew one day I would have to leave, not through choice, but through the death of my body. I had enjoyed the new feeling of growing up and the romance which started by engulfing my body, with incredible feelings and gradually left me in a state of utter contentment. Being happily married to a stunning beauty, who filled my life with so much purpose.

Eventually I had discharged myself from the irrelevant concerns of local people, and allowed myself the joy of being able to stroll through sweet smelling picturesque woods, and watch the effects of nature endorsing my soul with peace and fulfilment.

The lovely Cornish village, was superbly decorated with sparkling Christmas lights, and its atmosphere was staggering, with the effects of excitement by the young ones, soon to unwrap their presents. As time quickly moved on to the evening of Boxing Day, the family had gathered together for the annual party. I watched them from the chair, it made me feel my age, to see the young ones dance to that awful noise that passed for music. I felt fat and tired. It is funny how eating can tire you, or is it the noise, or

maybe meeting everyone, which makes the brain work overtime.

I was like the ancient one observing from a high celestial point. Every now and then, smiling to myself, at the antics of my younger relations. My daughter, herself a Grandmother, tapped my shoulder for the umpteen time, to see if I was alright. In a minute she will convince me I am not, but I am tired, I need to sleep for ever and ever, but not just yet.

It was at that junction, that the suggestion was placed, to visit the "Bull". So arrange ments were made, until the thought was voiced concerning the children. I solved that one, amazed how every molehill becomes a mountain at these get-togethers. Particular, as the oldest child was old enough to drive to the pub, but preferred to stay here, with her Sisters.

Great Granddad is going to tell a Cornish story to the children was voiced. Great Granddad, is that really me? I suppose 85 years would be long enough, but where did the years go? I had seen everybody here, grow up and face their individual problems. Was I satisfied with my life? That was twice reality had hit me tonight. Questions seemed to be pouring into my head, but no satisfying answers were jumping back. I stirred myself from the chair, to place a log in the fire. Funny how I feel so cold.

I sent the children to get changed into their night clothes. The noisy, excited party who were bound for the "Bull", left by the front door with shouts of "Good night" and "Go to bed at a reasonable time". Silence reigned for a short time, and I was left alone with my disturbing thoughts. But luckily it was not long before the other noisy, excited party descended the stairs, eager to hear my story.

As the youthful gang settled down to listen to the magical story, I led them down the road to explore the tales of King Arthur, and thought of explaining about the mystical sites that exist in Cornwall, but resisted, because this would be venturing too deep, and some were very young.

Our world operates on past, present and future factors, for the present is always changing and the past lingers in our mind but eventually will disappear. Hence the thought that time will eventually heal all disasters, seems right. While the future carries with it, an air of uncertainty, that can give you enthusiasm or for some desperation. For even the most obvious happenings can be changed by the future.

So on discovering sacred locations in Cornwall, it is obvious, what is visible is evident, although besides feeling the possibility of happenings that existed in time gone by, there are glimpses of other worlds, strategically in the background, that materialise themselves at certain times and operate on a different plane. For there are people with

with exceptional perceptions, that have the ability to report on these aspects which are outside our dimensions. But this can be difficult to comprehend, for many people are living in a life full of pressure and strain, and this apparition is outside their minds, and they just totally obliterate these thoughts, with themselves and their family.

So I decided to avoid going down the road of preaching, and just told a tale, that happened during the 1980s. There was a story presented that gave my thoughts some clarification, for a couple visiting Cornwall on holiday, searched and found what they believed was a King Arthur's building, which delighted them. Having journeyed away, though narrow mystic roads, they encounter a Village of pure enchantment. The view of the church and the cottages were very serene, and the whole area was totally peaceful and innocent, underneath a misty ray of glowing sunshine. It was several miles later, after departing from this atmospheric wonder, that they realised there was something alien about it, and after several minutes of consideration, it became obvious, there was no visual evidence of any living beings. So the couple returning on holiday again, explored the whole area and were unable to find it, which they found flabbergasting. Eventually, the couple moved to Cornwall as both were bewitched by the shimmering terrain, their meeting with one of their neighbours was amazing. For they were told the same story about a village the neighbours had seen only once, and now had spent many years trying to discover it again. So the village had become visible to this world, but had since dispersed to another plane, for which it appears back in this world when the spell specifies.

The children seemed to like the story, and now ventured off to bed, leaving me in a miserable, lonely state, missing my lovely wife, who had died several years before. I remember being able to sit with her in perfect contentment, with the feeling of happiness, of belonging, of a mind blowing relationship, how I wish she was here. However my mind was playing tricks, for before me was the beautiful lady, dressed in a long white flowing gown, her hand reached out for me. She seemed to be floating, and I moved towards her. My tiredness had gone, no aching bones, the feeling of total relaxation and peace rushed over my body. Just for a moment, I paused to look back and saw my body lifeless in the chair, but quickly continued towards the beautiful sight of my love. For now obviously, I would be unable to greet the New Year in, but the overwhelming excitement of returning with my exquisite love, to another plane, located in the hazy, veiled background of Sacred Cornwall, totally cleared my distress.

Robert Stephen Hawker

Morwenstow is situated in North Cornwall. The sea cliff is the highest on this coast, the dramatic setting is breath taking. The pounding of the crashing waves is an indication of how many shipwrecks have happened, for there is nothing but the sea between here and America. In the cliffs, is St Morwenna's Well, founded a long, long time ago, in the romantic spiritual past, by an early saint, named Morwenna, who was the daughter of the King of Wales, and travelled to Cornwall to devote herself to a religious way of life. Whether this legend is fact or fiction, is difficult to confirm, but where maybe the Saint cast her eyes upon the pulsating sea, was replicated, at a very later date, by Robert Stephen Hawker, whose outlook was lost in mystic reflection.

He first appeared there, on honeymoon, at the age of 19, after marrying a godmother, who was over 20 years older than him. He used the marriage to fund his Oxford University career, before moving to this area as a vicar for 41 years. He was a very talented person, who preached, worked, wrote poems about King Arthur, composed the song "Shall Trelawney Die", and set standards that was difficult for anyone else to approach. However being a remarkable person meant you were more likely to suffer from a time of despondency, and his wife, Charlotte, was able to help him through these periods, and even influence him back to those high levels.

Consequently, when his wife died at the age of 81, and was buried in Morwenstow, the vicar was devastated and overwhelmed with absolute grief, for her love had been a important part of his life, and now he was alone and depressed. The following year he married a second wife, and he become father to three daughters. However, as he approached his final years, his health declined seriously and was unable to cope with the problems of life, and on his death was buried in Plymouth, which seems difficult to comprehend, for someone who was a major influence in North Cornwall should be left in Devon. Although since then, several people have seen his spirit run free at Morwenstow, not inhibited by his human body, able to intermingle with the souls of others from time gone by. Hopefully he is able to spend time with his first wife, who gave him inspiration to be a genius, for he has, without doubt, left people with the indelible memory of "The Vicar of Morwenstow".

The Mermaid to the Rescue

He stood on top of a Cornish cliff, the view was magnificent, the sky totally blue except for the glowing, golden sunshine. A gentle warm breeze should have caused a stimulating realisation in his body. The white foaming waves were flowing in rhythmic delight, sea birds were gliding in the sky, there was an apparent peacefulness here, which should have been soothing for the soul. But unfortunately he was devastated with the torment relationship, with dare he say it, his wife. The irrelevant arguments are just so stupid, and she just goes on for hour after hour, about nothing, and the money she spends on sheer rubbish, makes her an absolute pain, particular as she earns nothing. But at the end of the day, he has 3 sons, aged 12, 10 and 8 years, who are the main part of his life, and no way would he want to hinder their growth, so he has no choice as he needs to be there for his family. So he considered jumping for a moment, but that would also hurt the progress of his sons, so how does he continue, for his mind is close to breaking.

Further along the cliffs, stood a graceful lady, who was crying and shaking, her partner had been to the pub and and as usual arrived home drunk, and ended hitting her, because he wanted sex and she stopped him. She had to get herself together, because her daughter was singing solo at school, this afternoon, and her other 3 daughters would need sorting. These were children from a first marriage, that ended when her husband ran away and she has yet to gain contact with him, so is unable to get maternity money. Although she has gained child benefit and income support, she never has time to work, because of looking after the youngsters. Therefore, she had to submit to a partner, to gain enough money. Which was a terrible way of looking at life, but at least it paid the mortgage and subsidised her dependents.

The two almost simultaneous looked at their watches and knew they had to go back, to rush around in totally constricted circles, and achieving what. Help and protection for their children, and what for themselves, maybe satisfaction for their souls. Sprinting back to their vehicles, they discovered an accident between 3 cars, which had blocked the exit to the car park, and the police were investigating. The two looked at each other, for the first time, not from their souls, but for help. They both needed to be back to St Ives, so the lady could attend school for the concert, and the man meet an appointed top rated client for his business. So walking to the main road, he was able, by mobile, to get one of his staff to pick them up quickly. On finding out where she lived, he would be able to return her car this afternoon, if that was alright. She just

26

agreed. She needed to hear her daughter sing, and have the car back before her partner arrived.

As time passed, so the two started to grow closer together, both needed someone to talk too, and tell their troubles, and were there to help each other. Eventually, the feeling of love for each other, engulfed them, and they became aware of the road, which might leave them in terrible trouble, for they were short of time, and to get further than daily telephone conversation was difficult.

Once or twice a month they managed to meet in a Cornish cove, hidden away from everyone else. Their souls were becoming inseparable, their encounter in this life was late, but they were sure they had been together in previous lives. They both wanted to be together for ever, but realised this could only happen when their children were grown up and were able to take on the world. So this relationship was giving them strength to continue to battle on, but it was making the sleeping with someone else, very difficult and stressful.

One day, as they met in the cove, the scene was serene. The warm breeze was shimmering through the pulsating white waves. Their eyes met with love, the touch of their hands, reinforce their souls. Suddenly, a shadow appeared on them, and they both looked around with apprehensive horror, for their togetherness was very obvious to a viewer. However they were astonished by the recognition of a very beautiful mermaid being there, whose conversation was very soothing, and she invited them to her home below the sea. She was able to help with the lack of oxygen and wet clothes, for shortly they arrived in an absolute paradise. Their minds had lost the pressure of life, the peacefulness was totally tranquil. Togetherness was exhilarating, speech was not necessary, for their souls pulsated each other.

Suddenly, they realised that time had elapsed, and they should have been back ages ago. However, when they looked at their watches, they were flabbergasted by the fact that both were not working. In anticipation of this problem, the mermaid was back, her words comforted them, for they were in a different plane, where there was not such a craze as time. The realities in this world was so different, and traditionally, it existed in the misty background of the human world, where people need the right perception in their minds to comprehend what is happening. For the couple had progressed far enough along the road to eternal light, to be able to visit this sanctuary.

Arriving back in the Cornish cove, they knew they could find a way to live together, in the very imminent future. Both felt so mentally and physically strong, stemming from their unique alliance, that gave them strength to take the world on. For they realised

how coming to discover the natural elements of Sacred Cornwall, had enrich their lives for ever.

Temple

The rhythmic sound of English thoroughbreds broke the early morning peace. The gentle breeze made eerie patterns with the hanging grey mist. The silver tips of the green grass hung low, heavy with the cold morning dew. A shimmering spider's web clung from the Norman apex of an archway, which marked the entrance to a small sacred Church.

Its stone had been hued from Cornish granite, the roofing slate mined from a quarry nearby. The Church had been built to withstand the fury of the elements created on this bleak part of Bodmin Moor.

A solitary figure, a man of God, stopped his pacing, and looked up to witness the approaching carriage. The urgent panting of the horses subsided as they concluded their frantic journey at the top of the winding path to the Church.

Two figures emerged from the carriage, their excited voices revealed their purpose, a quest of love. The head strong young man, determined to prove to his rich parents, that he was master of any situation. The pretty girl, with a disarming smile, held his hand, determined to hold his attention, and also to escape the inhuman cramped conditions of her parent's home, content to be carried away in a romantic dream.

This imaginary scene, probably happened in reality at the Church of Temple, which was the Cornish equivalent of Gretna Green, until the mid 1700 when an Act of Parliament was passed nullifying this loop hole.

The settlement of Temple was founded by the Knights Templars in the early 1100s. This order upheld the virtuous right of chivalry and worship, and established places of sanctuary all over Europe, for pilgrims and travellers journeying to the Holy Lands.

After losing its Gretna Green status, the Church fell into disrepair for more than a century, during which time the roof collapsed and killed a sheltering tramp. It was rebuilt in the mid 1800s on the existing foundations of the Church of the Knights Templar, retaining the original tower and incorporating many features of the old Church.

Today, Temple is no longer a refuge for the physical well being of the weary traveller, but emanating from the confines of the Church is an intrinsic interweaving of worship and love, a deeply rooted presence of an aura of peaceful tranquillity. The divine sun-

light filtering through the sacred window dedicated to St Catharine, descends directly from heaven.

This sanctuary of wonder offers an escape from the worldly pressures, by quiet meditation this haven of solitude invigorates the human spirit, restoring its hopes and dreams, allowing the spirit to continue its way along the eternal path to fulfilment.

Love is close, but yet so far away

The early morning light was gradually eroding the dark night in this Cornish village. The tuneful birds were launching their rhythmic singing. This was the time of year, that Spring was making its presence noticed, stimulating nature with everlasting delight.

Today, the wind had calmed down to a gentle breeze, swinging its way through leafless trees. The sky is clear, a thankful absence of rain, though previous days of heavy showers, had made the streams expand into fast flowing rivers, that collided with the salt water of the ever busy sea.

The sun's rays were filtering through the frosty windows of my cottage, making my rooms glow with appealing illumination, although this had no effect on me, because I had no purpose in life. On leaving my comfortable abode for an adventuresome walk, to generate some reason for living, I noticed the earth seemed very alive. Strolling for many hours, I eventually discovered a secret, secluded Cornish cove, the misty sequence made this location so very different.

Standing alone on a tranquil sandy beach, the view out to sea was breathtaking, for where I was, seemed in another world of total wonder and amazement. The area was sending waves of romantic feeling, for love was very apparent, an emotion, I was missing. I have never seen a lady to adore, never needed to filter myself into her spirit of wonder.

The glowing sun was bright and refreshing all of nature's beings, it was giving the world a reason for living, and overcoming all the adversity that could present itself. Softly the breeze brought myself, a feeling of total contentment. The eternal light was closer, a shadow appeared at my feet, the uttering of emotion was rushing into my heart. This world was shimmering into a cluster of twilight, the shadow became a reality, for before me, was an angelic lady of glowing beauty.

As our eyes met, there was an instance recognition of her soul. My whole body vibrated with amazing excitement, for the glorious memory which was stirring deep in my

soul, showed we were far from being strangers. Her voice was soothing, as she told me, of our previous lives together, the many necessary encounters that was helping us along the path to the eternal light. So far in our present lives, we had been apart in different worlds, yet for this moment the two worlds had filtered together, allowing us to remember and enjoy our timeless love, which will help us to progress through our seemingly, pointless, present existence.

Our hands touched, our souls were as one, our kissing brought out, our physical need for each other. I revealed, how much I loved her, and we were lost in each others charms, far away from the present worlds, in a time of beautiful, exquisite, scintillating passion.

In the aftermath, as peace and tranquillity, soothed our souls, I desperately needed to remain with her, but slowly there was a flickering that started to draw the worlds apart. We gradually started to disappear from each other, despite our determined efforts to stay together. The lady was gone. For a minute I stopped, and started to feel bitterly upset, and even began to think, was that a dream or was it reality.

However, the lady's overwhelming love has given me such breath-taking strength. It had left in my mind, the concept of how our love could overcome everything, if we both followed the right path of life. For today, I have been given the key to unlock the secrets in my soul, and there is no doubt, that in the future, we were destined to be inseparable.

But when would we be back together again? This life or the next? When would that other world filter itself back into Sacred Cornwall? This has emerged as my ultimate need. My future was indeed heading for paradise, but I will just have to wait patiently, lingering in the exquisite influence of my feelings, induced by the memory of the beautiful lady's shimmering soul.

Therefore, at the end of the day, when all is said and done, Sacred Cornwall has helped me find a reason for living, and there is no doubt, it is a divine heavenly abode definitely superior to all others.

Special Thanks to:-

The Paul Watts Cornish Picture Library for supplying the images.
Cornish Lithographic Printers for their printing and finishing.

Published by:-

R & B Enterprise, Trelawney Lodge, Keveral Lane, Seaton, Cornwall PL11 3JJ
Telephone 01503 250673 Fax 01503 250383
Written by Roger Lock. Design by Barbara Lock.
Supportive work by Barbara Davis.
© Roger Lock 2004   ISBN 0-9544335-1-3

Sacred Cornwall - The Heritage

First book in the series, full of facts, myths and legends, including stories of Jesus, John Wesley, King Arthur, St Michael's Ley Line, Kings Templar, The Mermaid of Zennor and The Reason for Living
Available at most Book Shops and Tourist Information Centres, but if unable to find, please ring 01503 250673.